AYA

A Y A

Okornore Manu

AYA

Copyright © Okonore Manu, 2019
All Rights Reserved

This book is sold subject to the condition that it shall not, by way of trade of otherwise, be lent, re-sold, hired out or otherwise circulated without the publisher's prior consent, in any form of binding or cover other than that in which it is published and without a similar condition including this condition being imposed on the subsequent purchaser.

No part of this book may be reproduced in any form by photocopying or by any electronic or mechanical means, including information storage in a retrieval system, without the written permission of both the copyright owner and the publisher of this book.

ISBN: 978 9988 8904 6 9
ABAVANNA SERIES (AV11)

Cover Design and Book Layout by
Nene Buer Boyetey
P O Box NM 78, Nima, Accra, Ghana
Email: nene@bigglesglobal.com
Tel: +233 302 333 502 | +233 244 634 204

Published by
DAkpabli & Associates
P O Box 7465, Accra North, Accra, Ghana
Email: info@dakpabli.com
Tel: +233 264 339 066 | +233 244 704 250 | +233 247 896 375

AUTHOR'S PROFILE

Okornore strives for empathy; not for the sake of altruism, but because life is pretty much a pot of spoiled beans for everyone in her generation, and it can only be a good thing if we were all a little kinder and were willing to be more vulnerable. Plus, using stories to make others feel seen makes her feel warm and fuzzy inside.

This sentiment is the cause of Okornore's incessant oversharing, which often has to be dressed up in poetry and prose in the spirit of serving medicine with a spoonful of sugar.

In *Aya*, Okornore explores themes of loss, ambivalence, anger, confusion and a certain brand of healing, that often presents as madness to the untrained eye.

DEDICATION

For those who need to find respite in vulnerability, because it can be such a rarity in our world.

For Serwah; you never had a chance to experience this life, but I'd like to imagine that these are the kinds of stories I would have guided you through life with.

For Tara and Nana Ama.

ACKNOWLEDGEMENTS

During my time at university, I often wondered if I should continue writing. I would like to thank Matthias Asiedu-Yeboa, for no other reason but being who he is – an encourager and someone who sees almost everything as something that can be saved. The same goes for Poetyk Prynx, who is one of the bravest poets I know and my own personal groupie.

I would also like to thank my cousin Georgia Frimpong, who has always seen and appreciated me as a creative and would hype my poetry to her friends long before I even considered that I might have an audience that wants to read what I write.

Thanks also to anyone who bought my first book and received it well, despite what it was. You encouraged me to go for better.

All my friends in Accra's creative space – more vim!

CONTENTS

Aya

'Fern'

"An individual who wears this symbol suggests that [they have] endured many adversities and outlasted much difficulty."

–Willis, 1998, The *Adinkra* Dictionary

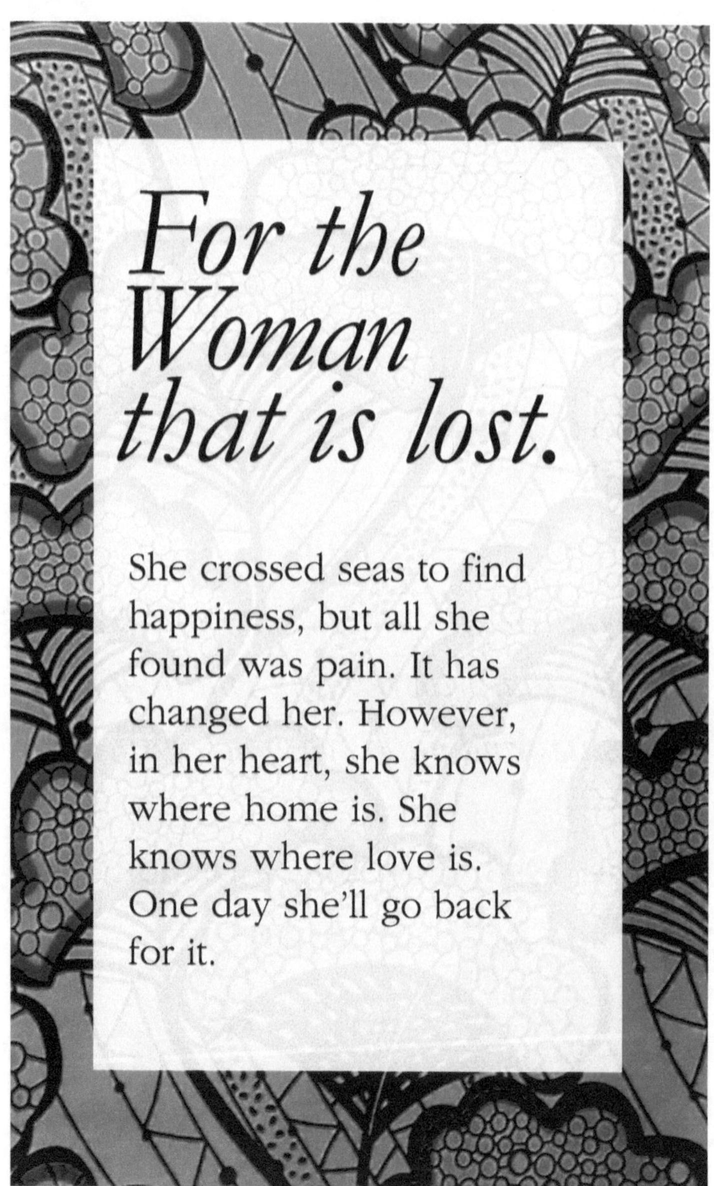

For the
Woman
that is lost.

She crossed seas to find
happiness, but all she
found was pain. It has
changed her. However,
in her heart, she knows
where home is. She
knows where love is.
One day she'll go back
for it.

FALL

The rain soothes me.

A bit like your words
when you call me your love.

Puddles make me think whether your feels are as
deep as the middle of the ocean
Or as rough as the waves at shore.

Are you the beach at ebb time, where I, a shipwreck,
finds solace in the shallow waters?
Or will your tide rock me into place?
Is this a new journey?

The drone of showers is your voice when it gives me
chills in the morning.

I listen, quietly.
Like when your words fall on my ears,
the earth swallows rain up quickly
and makes things muddy.

Inevitably, this will end.
Till then, I will listen to the rain
I will listen to it sing of you.

SOUL FOOD

Akara Recipe

A cup of peeled beans
One chilli pepper
Red bell pepper
Spring onions
Flour
Salt
Paprika powder

First, soak the beans overnight (do not skip this part — you will regret it However, also do not let your beans sit in water for a week)

When you're ready, cut off the bulbs of your spring onion (the white part) from the greens. Put the bulbs in the blender, add your chilli.

Drain and rinse the beans. Add them to the other ingredients and fill up the blender with enough water to just cover the beans.

When blended smooth, pour mixture into bowl — add flour and mix

Add chopped onion greens, peppers and whip (I know you don't own a whip — use a fork)

Finally add salt to taste and paprika (my secret ingredient)

Ajoke smiled as she typed out the lie about the paprika.

Ajoke closed her browser, then her laptop and lifted herself from the same highchair she sits at every morning for breakfast. The island is one of her favourite things about her kitchen. The smooth azure surface reminds her of home.

The kitchen was Ajoke's favourite place in general. She's always loved to cook, so her friends often asked her for recipes, no matter how many times she told them that she mostly just wings it, like every other black woman. When her white friends ask, she sometimes obliges, because honestly, she'd rather send them a haphazard email with everything they could have found on Google, rather than invite them to her house and demonstrate. It's one thing to have strangers in the kitchen when she runs cooking classes, but it's less desirable in her home. She actually can't think of anything more foreign than a white person in her kitchen, asking about spices their ancestors should have taught them to use – seeing that they stole them and all that jazz.

As Ajoke approaches the stove, the *knister* and low bubble of her stew reaches her ears. All the hairs on her body erect a little. Things seem to slow down in motion and she can clearly visualise the thin stream of steam escape from the eye of the pot lid. When she is close enough, she watches the vapour some more, before shifting her gaze slightly to the splatters of red on the inside of the glass lid. Ajoke's pots are older than she is, but they are in pristine condition. On the top of her cabinets are boxes upon boxes of crockery that she has received as gifts, but she continues to use her mother's pots. She considered throwing them out when her mother died, but she doesn't associate the pots with her mother as much as she associates them with her childhood and her own love for food. Ajoke has cooked many a meal for loved ones in these pots. When the thought of overhauling her kitchenware came to her, she just decided that she won't let her hate for her mother get in the way of her affection towards these pots. After all, she completely redid the kitchen that her mother spent most of her time in. The canvas was different – Ajoke assured herself that using the same brushes was ok.

It was almost time for her guests to arrive, so she went to her dining room to set the table. The place where she hosted most of her dinner parties, was more like an extension of the house than just a room. The area was large and colourful. To one side the wall was almost completely glass, so her guests could look out into the garden which flourished throughout the year. Ajoke's guests often asked her how she got certain plants to fruit out of season and without fail, she would divert the conversation to another topic. How tightly Ajoke protects her food secrets has become a running joke amongst her friends, but she didn't mind as long as none of them cared enough to press the matter further. She had the dining area built with the money she received from sympathisers at her mother's funeral. At first, it was a way to spite her mother.

Growing up, Ajoke always ate on the kitchen floor, or on the step leading into the backyard. Often, she watched as her mother would serve the food to her rich, mostly male, guests. In preparation for each of these dinners that her mother hosted, Ajoke had to polish silverware till she could see herself in the shiny surfaces – her mother wanted everything to be perfect. While Ajoke's mother knew she would inevitably get what she wanted from her guests through her charm, she wanted the act to seem believable.

Yayra was a smart woman who hated nothing more than to hear her neighbours calling her a witch. So, to avoid this, she spent years developing her dinners into an experience that came close to making it understandable that her guests would write her enormous checks as soon as they had finished dinner. When patrons from her chop bar came to gift her generators, cartons of produce and even the 4x4 that was now beat up and parked in the driveway, all Yayra would say is that her god was repaying her kindness to hungry people.

Ajoke admired her mother's generosity to beggars but hated her neglecting her daughter for money. Ajoke hated it even more when her friends at school would call her a witch, because she knew this was true. She spent most of her teen years annoyed at her mother's theatrics for the main reason that she wasn't fooling anybody. Once, one of Yayra's suitors came to the house to drop a check but Ajoke was the only one at home.

"Hm, this your mother. She has charmed me. I know she is a marine spirit. She thinks we don't know that she crawled out of a river", the man went on as he put his signature on the check.

"My wife's prophet saw it in a dream. Yayra is just lucky that some things do not bother me."

Ajoke stared at the man with her lips turned down in disgust. Her eyes, sizing him up repeatedly. He wasn't a bad looking man. His agbada was sharp, his shoes were shined to perfection. He could probably get a girl of Ajoke's age to fall for his charisma, but nothing could compete with Yayra's beauty or power.

"Now that all my smallies have left me, shey you people will now be the ones to enjoy my money. She should be happy. Me sef, I'm happy – the small girls were too stressful."

The man let out a wry laugh and looked at Ajoke to join in as his arm stretched out to her, but she just stared at him and took the check from his hand. When he had left, Ajoke looked at the figure on the check and it was enough to cover her school fees and get her some new school shoes. Her mother wasn't stingy, so Ajoke spent the rest of the day thinking of other things she might like.

When Yayra died, there was nothing left. In their last conversation, Yayra told her daughter that things might temporarily get hard, but Ajoke was to make sure she used her own gift to manage herself. Ajoke wasn't sure what to expect, so when she looked in her mother's bank account and it was empty, she almost threw up. Luckily for her, some of her mother's chop bar customers never realised that the food they ate put them under a spell. At a point, they were gifting Yayra things for the sake of it, because it had become the habit and when she died, Ajoke was awoken from sleep every dawn by sympathisers bringing her condolence gifts.

Now, Ajoke had her own diners. Once a month she would hold a supper club and she also did a lot of food blogging. Her guests often bring her small gifts, but she is sure it's out of courtesy. Ajoke wants her guests to leave richer than they came and as long as they ate her special akara, they always did.

TEMPEST

Naked, and slave to the rain, I lie in a cotton field dreaming of you.

My mind screams for you; the scars you carry.
The ones I couldn't heal.

Naked, and slave to the rain, my tears are drowned out by the heavens.

I dare not move as the ground swallows me up.
I am dying with my eyes wide open.

The journey here was like punishment for seven lives worth of sin.

But I didn't deserve it in this one.

Not in this life that I had kept myself for you.

In my last life my morals were decayed.

I laid with anyone; I lied and stole souls

In that life I would have accepted this fate but now…

I refuse to decay into dust before life springs from me.

So, I shake off the mud before the sound of the carriage carrying you away goes silent.

I love you, but I will not die for you.

I am a weed that is strong and stubborn and will starve that which is beautiful to survive.

The seed you left in me will grow, and its seeds will spread with the bees to find you.

They will tell you how their mother birthed a dream of freedom.

In the middle of a cotton field.

In the eye of the storm.

You know me, so you'll know what they say is true.

Through the tempest, your seed will find you.

JOURNEY TO THE WEST

Part One

A warm draft flutters the torn edge of window netting in Wendy's room. As she stands, legs wide apart amid yam, gari and dried fish, she fans herself with a corner of the worn out Vlisco cloth hanging around her neck. It's impossible to tell whether Wendy is traveling or trying to stock a supermarket with the contents of the suitcases on the floor. There's an acquired scent lingering in the room; a combination of the fish, wrapped in brown paper and the stale water festering in the gutter behind her bedroom. The whirring of thousands of mosquitoes is inaudible unless focused on. A coil to deter them idly blows smoke ringlets in the corner.

"I for buy Peak Milk?" Wendy asks.

She is looking in the mirror on her dresser, admiring her small facial features and slanted eyes. Wendy's chocolate complexion was only blemished by a few scab marks on elbows and knees from childhood adventures. Adventures she was usually coerced into by her cousin. Wendy hated adventures but Naa loved them, so Wendy went along until she ended up loving them, too.

The small wireless radio that used to belong to Wendy's mother provides ambiance and as soon as the beat drops on Beyoncé's Déjà Vu, Wendy grabs a rat tail comb from the dresser. She turns the music up with no regard for the fact that it's 11 pm and her uncle is asleep down the hall. With her makeshift microphone at hand, it's as though Wendy has teleported to a different world – one with spotlights and paparazzi. She mimes the words of the song perfectly and wades through imaginary zebra grass in true Beyoncé fashion while leaving the mounds of goods on the ground undisturbed.

Sitting on the bed, Naa admires the bounce in Wendy's natural mane as she twirls around the room and mimics the routine from the music video. Wendy's flowy nightdress only makes her theatrics more believable. She genuinely looks lovelorn in the way she passionately grabs her head and reaches out to Naa with shaky hands, suggesting a love induced delirium. Naa usually lives for these performances by Wendy but today, watching her causes a knot in Naa's throat.

It's not long before Wendy is tired and stops to catch her breath. She leans her head back, inhales deeply and is filled with joy. She supports her lower back with one hand and rests the other on her tummy as baby feet kick against her skin from the inside. Wendy chuckles with content and looks at Naa, waiting for an ovation she doesn't receive. Instead, Naa just stares at her.

"They have Nido in London." Naa answers Wendy's question curtly.

Wendy looks at Naa as if to say "Really? That's how you're going to be?" and goes back to packing her things while humming along to the R&B song that's now playing.

"You're coming home with Jason when he's here for Christmas anyway, right? It's not like you'll have time to miss it even if you can't get any," Naa continues.

"I'll be ready to pop by then. I'm not getting on a plane in that state," Wendy replies in a purposefully bland tone and without looking up from her task of packing.

"So, when next am I seeing you?" The mixture of frustration and anger in Naa's tone pierces Wendy and she turns to face Naa dead on.

"Naa, I do not know."

There's a silence. The two women just stare at each other hesitantly – both encountering a new level of adulting and not quite knowing how to navigate this. They have never been apart.

"Ama, are you sure you are ready to leave?" Naa asks, fumbling around the awkwardness.

Wendy sits on the edge of the bed, facing away from Naa and bows her head as a form of surrender. She covers her face as she starts crying, suddenly, but doesn't try to control her sobs.

"We've been together ever since your parents died, Ama. I know dad gives you hell over the pregnancy, but I'll be done with school soon and then I can help with money." Naa whispers in a soothing, reassuring manner.

Wendy scoffs and shakes her head. "You don't even believe the three of us could live on a graduate job salary yourself. Where are the jobs, even?"

Naa has no response. All her sisters married young or had kids with wealthy guys to avoid the struggle of the Accra job market. Why should Wendy be any different?

"In London I'll be able to get a gig or two – Jason says he knows some producers looking for new acting talent," Wendy adds.

"Ugh, everyday Jason." Naa explodes. "Can you not see he's a sleazy dirt bag? Everyone knows he's a *Sakawa* boy – your soul is probably in a calabash under his bed. Normal people don't get rich overnight like that."

"Sakawa boys do fraud, not *Juju*." Wendy replies; exhausted. She's stopped crying, but Wendy's cheekiness irritates Naa.

"Jason has accepted this child. He didn't have to. After you told your dad how all of this happened, and he went to Jason all guns blazing, I thought that was it but he's taking me to London. It's all going to be fine." Wendy tries to reason.

Naa sighs, dries her own tears and hugs her cousin tightly from behind. She buries her face in Wendy's hair, inhaling deeply. Wendy smelt of everything lovely. Of coconut and mango; affection and warmth – Wendy smelt like home to Naa.

"*Mi sumo bo* – don't ever forget that."

Wendy sighs deeply.

Part Two

As Wendy walks out of the gynaecology department at St Thomas' Hospital she makes her way to the car park as fast as she possibly can.

Wendy unlocks her Mercedes GLE Coupe and impatiently paces towards it. Open-toed Louboutin shoes aren't exactly convenient to walk in and hospitals made her itch. With every step, Wendy seems to be getting angrier as though balancing on six inches has suddenly become the biggest inconvenience imaginable. The icy weather doesn't help either. She's only been outside for a few moments, but the breeze wraps itself around her exposed feet and makes her nose run.

Wendy's breathing gets heavier with every step. She

flings the car door open in half anger, half relief and slumps into the driver's seat. She closes the door and exhales deeply. With her eyes closed, she imagines breathing out pain and tension and anxiety. She holds her breath for a few moments in a quest to postpone what will happen next.

Saliva gathers in Wendy's mouth; her chest gets tight as her lungs fight for her to respond to impulse. Wendy's mind, however, is calm and she can feel her blood pressure drop. Her muscles relax but unfortunately, just as she feels the effects she was trying to achieve, she is forced to inhale. Wendy breathes all her hard feelings back in and they exit again through uncontrollable tears. Within moments, Wendy finds herself in a hot pot of emotions that were just being recycled over and over. She is hyperventilating. Wendy opens the door and steps out, gasping for fresh air. Once she's a little calmed, Wendy gets back in. Unsure about where to go, Wendy sparks the ignition.

Wendy drives into the heart of South London. As she approaches Brixton, she experiences the phantom sensation of smelling freshly baked sweet bread and it makes her smile wistfully. Wendy decides to stop at the market. She'd lived in London for several years now and had driven past it before, but she had always been with Jason and never actually entered. The most she could hope for was to smell fresh bread. Even in passing, the stall right at the mouth of the market always made her happy. In between an

Iceland Foods and a Boots Pharmacy nestled a small stall of fruit and vegetables. Incidentally, every time Wendy had driven past, this stall had mangoes on display. Not the Spanish kind she sees in Tesco. Wendy often ogled the yellowy orange fruit, displayed in straw filled crates, wondering how her tree back home is faring.

Once she's found somewhere to park, Wendy walks into the market and suddenly the grey skies no longer mattered. The bright lights from the stalls and shops tickled her into a broad smile. As she passed an oriental shop that displayed fresh crabs, she rubs the shell of one whilst the shopkeeper isn't looking and is invigorated by the cold, rough touch. Her senses were having a field day, but Wendy decides to move on swiftly so as not to attract attention. She already stands out against the other shoppers, mainly women in colourful leggings and thick coats. The young girls stare at her hair which almost reaches her bottom now that she's chemically straightened it and she stares back at their nappy hair tied up in adorable buns. She enters a shop that looks like a butcher's shop at first glance, but Wendy spotted the shelf of bread in the back from outside. She smiles at the men behind the meat counter and one winks at her. After picking up a loaf, she hands him a twenty-pound note and walks out without a word, but she catches the blessings of prosperity from various gods they rain on her.

Wendy not only missed sweet bread but also the

hustle and bustle of women haggling over plantain and cassava. The pavement in Brixton market is uneven and speckled with pot holes, very much like Kaneshie. There are puddles of grey matter framing the rainbow of okra, scotch bonnets, red snapper, aubergines and the likes. Men in white cloaks cat call and flirt with customers to make that extra sale on cow foot – their pitch not too different from Fan Ice hawkers in Achimota traffic.

 On her way back Wendy walks past a corner shop and notices a birthday card on display. It's rather large and old fashioned but the image of two little black girls playing with a dog appeals to her and she buys it.

Wendy doesn't go straight home. She drives into Streatham and turns into a side street just before she reaches the park. Streatham Common Park held a lot of beautiful memories of the early days in Wendy's marriage. Jason would watch her from the benches as he socialised with his partners and Wendy took walks with their wives while they cooed over her bump. Wendy was here for a different purpose though. She drives up to a building that used to be a church and ruffles about in her glove compartment for the keys. Once inside, the building feels abandoned at first but as soon as she switches the lights on she is hugged by inexplicable warmth. Wendy walks through a high arch, into the main hall.

The stone floors protest against Wendy's shoes with

echoing clicks and clacks so she takes them off. Once before the altar, she kneels and recites a few Hail Marys. Wendy soaks in the clarity that comes with the peace she's experiencing. Since the first day, Jason brought Wendy here after buying the building she's had visions every time she sat at the altar; A dance school maybe or theatre. Wendy loved these visions but they come to her much rarer than they used to. She considers what would have happened if she had found out today that she was pregnant again and then decides to find solace in pouring out her heart into a dreary birthday card.

Part Three

Wendy arrives at her apartment's valet station late and tired from the emotional roller coaster that the day has been. As she approaches, the elder of the building's valet team welcomes her. He's a pudgy man, with a permanently blank expression, old enough to be Wendy's father.

"Hi, Mr Jameson."

"Good evening Mrs…. good evening Ms." Mr Jameson responds curtly.

 Wendy smiles, gets her bag and the loaf and is about to exit the car but Mr Jameson is standing right in front of the door.

He doesn't budge even when Wendy looks at him quizzically, "Mr Billz has been looking for you, Ms."

"Oh." Wendy replies letting her expression drop.

"If I may be honest, Mr Billz has been – for want of a better phrase – quite the nuisance."

"I see." Wendy looks away.

Mr Jameson looks at Wendy silently in contemplation and then continues, "Ms, I believe Mr Billz is having one of his moments."

Wendy turns to look at Mr Jameson again and forces a smile which isn't reciprocated.

"Well...first of all, Mr Jameson, you know you can call him Mr Asare, right? And I keep telling you to call me Ama – our relationship is hardly professional anymore. You've seen me on some of my worst days, you're practically family."

"I shall escort you upstairs then – carry your shopping." Mr Jameson responds.

Wendy chuckles but this time with genuine appreciation towards Mr Jameson's concern, "Thanks, Mr Jameson, but I think I can carry this heavy load myself." She responds, partly in jest.
Mr Jameson watches Wendy skeptically as she gets out of the car but he doesn't insist further. As she

walks past him, she pats him on the shoulder and his expression softens.

Wendy enters the hallway of her twelfth floor flat and can see Jason standing by the windows in the living room. The flat is only illuminated by the bright lights of the city. The place is filled with smoke which makes Wendy dizzy. She stands and watches him uncertainly for a few moments and then quietly makes for the bedroom.

"There's was no dinner," Jason shouts to her from two rooms away.

Wendy rolls her eyes as she drops her bag on the bed and begins to undress while observing the stillness of the Thames through the bedroom window. When she turns around, Jason is standing in the room. Startled, Wendy takes a step back.

"Did you hear me, Wendy? Why wasn't there dinner? There's been no food all day." Jason speaks calmly now. He moves slowly and the shadows in the room dance on his face.

Wendy can feel goose bumps growing on her skin and her mouth dries up. Jason is still speaking to her, but his words are tuned out by her brain trying to assess the room for escape routes.

Jason raises his voice again, "Why you naked?"

Wendy looks down at herself – she's still wearing underwear but slowly approaches the bed, so she can reach for a bed sheet. As she covers her body with one corner and tugs to free up more her hands shake, and she never takes her gaze of Jason who is pacing about the room.

"You think you're hot init? That's why you think you can do whatever you want?" Jason barks, "Look at you all gaunt – skin looking all mash up. You're a ugly bitch – you fuckin' cunt… bitch." As he waves his hand at Wendy dismissively, he staggers to the side, leans his forehead against the wall and takes a puff from his joint.

"You did this to me, Jason." Wendy says almost inaudibly interrupting a Hail Mary.

Jason turns his head slightly and grimaces, "What?" Wendy braces herself against close-by furniture, anxiously trying to shimmy into an advantageous position to dart across the bed and into the bathroom. "You're a sick piece of shit, and you need help." Wendy's voice crescendos and climaxes on the last word.

Jason turns around and Wendy tightly grips the bedsheet she's wrapped around her and closes her eyes to focus her.

"Look … Jason … it's late, ok. I'm sorry about what I said." Jason doesn't respond, just stares. "I should have been home to cook dinner." Tears start to well in Wendy's eyes, "Let me get something to wear from the closet and I'll go fix you something, ok?"

With eyes open again, Wendy approaches her walk-in closet and hears his steps approaching. Wendy runs into the far corner of the room and curls up into a ball to protect most of her body.

Jason crouches down to her level and grabs her face, forcing Wendy to look him. The smell of alcohol, weed and sweat seeping from him is making Wendy sick. Behind Jason, on a drawer chest, stands a collection of Wendy's pictures. No pictures of Wendy as Ama are displayed anywhere else, just this little shrine in her closet. A photo of her and Naa at the beach catches her eye. Jason observes Wendy's face as she zones out. Naa's face is puffy because Wendy had pretended to be drowning and Naa cried her eyes out because she couldn't swim. It was a bet; some of the other kids wanted to know if Naa would ever cry. Naa didn't cry at her mother's funeral and everyone was certain that she wouldn't cry for Wendy.

The sound of Jason's belt buckle being undone jolts Wendy out of reminiscence. Her heart is racing, and her palms are sweaty. She gropes around the shelf behind her for something that could do some damage while Jason is distracted with his trouser buttons. Wendy grabs a wedge boot and as Jason lowers himself over her, she smacks him across the face with the heel and bolts out of the closet picking up her bag on the way.

Wendy finds her phone and dials a number. As the phone rings Wendy can't keep the tears in anymore. When the person on the other end picks up Wendy doesn't speak – she just sobs uncontrollably. Leaning against the door, she can feel Jason kicking against it and she's sure the expletives he's hurling at her are audible through the phone line. Muffled sobs are all that Wendy can produce until the doorbell rings.

"Thank you."

"Don't worry Ama. You'll be ok."

Part Four

Thanks to Naa, the Barnor family home had an entire room dedicated to books. Where she lacked in interest for boys, she had made up with her love for literature.

Every Saturday Jane, the nurse, passes by the library to borrow a new book to read to Naa. Naa's home collection may have been vast, but Jane rattled through it in the first few weeks on the job as reading them to Naa was the only way Naa could be calmed after night terrors. Sometimes, Jane also passes by the post office to check Naa's PO Box. This was one of those Saturdays, but it was extra special, so Jane also brought cake. When she arrives at the house, almost skipping through the compound, she greets the gardener and shares petty gist with the laundry lady who is also the cook.

The house is the brightest in the area. Along the line, someone thought it a clever idea to have it painted green in its entirety. To match the house, the gardener perfectly maintains the glorious landscape which includes a small vegetable garden and he takes immense pride in the mango tree up front. The pool is always clean although no one ever swims in it and the cars in the driveway that have become mainly decorative are waxed regularly to give the security guard something to do.

The longer Jane works here the more she envies the staff that get to spend their time outdoors or in the staff quarters. The bond she now has with Naa and her salary are her only consolation. Jane regularly imagines how the big, marbled, echoing rooms could look heavenly if it wasn't for the eerie sight of a bloody depiction of Jesus in the darkened living room. It creeps her out every single time.

Jane often thought that Naa's condition had invited evil into the house and she was only reassured by the various Christian emblems, except the Jesus portrait, for protection. Jane believes in amulets and trinkets of all kinds, but none worked for Naa. She just stews in the negativity. Even on the rare good days that Naa leaves her bedroom or speaks, Jane knows she'll be back tomorrow to find her regressing again.

Today isn't one of the good days. Jane can hardly find her way around Naa's room. It seems like she had the help drape even more sheets over the windows. When Jane goes to check, a rough plywood sheet blocking every source of natural light almost gives her a splinter. Jane dips in self-pity for a moment about the fact that she hasn't been able to make Naa get better, but she is not one to give up. Jane finds some candles and match sticks with the help of her phone screen light.

Jane tidies up the room, fetches water from the en-suite with the help of one of the candles and towel bathes Naa. Naa remains very calm, almost asleep, through it all. Sometimes she opens her eyes, confused, as though she was expecting to be somewhere else – with someone different. Naa whispers something incoherent while Jane goes about her job and she assumes that Naa is calling for Ama again. It is always as if Naa was trying to warn her about something. As far as Jane was concerned, Wendy is perfectly safe. What more could one want than to be living abroad with a rich husband?

Wendy always made sure Jane and the other staff are paid – sometimes with a bonus here and there. Jane always assumed Wendy was a lawyer or a businesswoman with her own boutique and at least a dozen maids. She didn't understand why she never came to visit Naa, but she had seen such things before. When people travel abroad and become too busy or can't come home because the water would

make them sick. At least, Wendy takes care of Naa –
and she writes every now and again. Naa's reactions
to Wendy's letters vary so Jane isn't sure whether to
read the card she'd collected but now Jane decides
to.

Once Naa is clean and had eaten, Jane gathers most
of the candles around Naa's bed and sits on the edge
with the card. Jane smiles at the effort Wendy put into
these things. She stares at Naa for a moment and
reaches out to tuck one of her bouncy twists behind
her ear.

Happy Birthday Naa,

*I hope the card gets to you in time. Before I say anything, I just want
you to know that I still love you. You're more than a sister to me and
you always will be.*

*I'm also sorry. I'll always be sorry - mainly for leaving you. I'm not
always sure things would have been better had I stayed but maybe I
was simply being selfish. I wouldn't blame you if you never wanted to
see me again, but it would be nice to be together.*

*I feel like I sold myself and I feel like I sold you, too. He couldn't have
hurt you if I hadn't let him in. Or at least, if I had come home with
him. Or not told him to stay at our house. I'm sorry I didn't believe
you.*

He raped you and I didn't do anything.
Jane is intrigued – she was never really told what

caused Naa's trauma. She also wasn't expecting this kind of a message inside a birthday card and it all didn't sound anything like Wendy.

I know you don't talk about it, but I look at the bruises and scars from him and they aren't as many as the ones I share with you.
I've often thought of dying but then I think I'd be killing the part of your soul that's still left.

I miss you Naa.

Mi sumo bo,

Ama

Jane thinks to herself how Wendy always stays true to signing off with "I love you". Jane doesn't speak Ga, but love has a weird way of transcending logic and being understood.

Jane notices there's a PS at the very bottom of the card. She tries to read it out but is stuck.

"Naa, look," Jane touches Naa's arm and feels her body slightly trembling.

The whole time Jane had been so engrossed in the card that she didn't notice Naa had started crying.

"Oh, Naa," Jane has never seen Naa cry. She's seen her angry and frustrated but never crying. Jane gives Naa a hug and only realises it is inappropriate once it's too late. Naa didn't mind – she let Jane's hair caress her face.

Jane shows Naa the note on the card. "Look. What does this say? *M…Mi ba…*"

Naa's eyes look confused as soon as she realises what it says. She looks at Jane for clarity who in turn is waiting for Naa to translate. Naa grabs the envelope from Jane's lap and inspects it. The tears running down her face getting more intense.

"When did she send this?"

Jane is taken aback at the first words Naa has spoken to her in a very long time.

"Erm, I don't know. A few weeks ago, I guess. I haven't checked the post box in a while. What does the note say, Naa?"

Naa can't control the tears anymore and sobs loudly as she cups her face with her hands.

"Oh, Naa, what does it say?"

It takes Naa a while to get herself together and catch her breath.

"Mi nba shia."

Naa sits back and looks at Jane with a grand smile on her face.

"She's coming home."

PINKIE PROMISE

I promise
on everything I hold dear
that it's ok for you to love me

yes, it's fine for you to watch me when I slumber
you can cook for me and I'll actually eat it

if you want, I'll let you touch me
we'll cut out the sex and you can just caress me
I'll let you stroke my hands, even though they're
most sensitive

we can hold hands in public
you can introduce me to your friends
and I'll introduce you to my God

we'll talk about children and our parents
I'll tell you about my father if you ask
I promise, one day I'll ask you to teach me your
mother tongue

when we're alone I won't play music to drown you
out
I promise I'll listen to our hearts synchronising
no more hiding

I'll tell you all that happened
and I'll cry – don't think that I won't
I'll let you put seams in my open cuts

I'll be naked and maybe I'll put on candles
I'll kiss you because now it's ok

now it's ok

I'll say I love you and only care a little bit who hears
I promise I'll be what I didn't let you ask of me
I'll be me in my entirety

I'll love me enough to love you
I promise

For the Queen *that no longer has her Crown.*

She spends every day trying to get back to her throne. She worships the gods inside her even when they torment her – she knows that they are a reality she must face. Her children are gifted. Not every seed inside of her bares the fruit she wants but she knows that she will bloom in due time.

DEW

Yesterday, I was dull and dry
I frayed raffia mats that were laid on my skin
I bled beasts that could no longer stew in my heat

I was rough and tired
So brittle, that I cracked under the word 'ugly'
Today, that's no longer true

You came and now I bear fruit again
My crevices are filled with your morning dew and I
am malleable
You use me to patch up the voids in your home

The climax of our love; only temporary
Yet, you reminded me what it's like to be tickled
As you trickled through my withered garden and
made me bloom

Your storm brings back memories of a former life
and I dissolve in you
I drown myself and become your vessel
Until the sun comes up and you rise above me

ALA'S DAUGHTERS

Death

It was a misty dawn and the air was filled with the thick sickening smell of desolation. Red dirt had been whirled into her hut by the winds of rage and now it settled between her toes. She watched the ground be still again as the raffia curtain flapped in an eerie breeze, blowing into the hut. She wishes the stillness had been one of peace for the living and not for the dead.

Eventually, the others began to stir while she remained caked against the wall of her hut; her aura sparkling in the dimness. Ana watched blood crawl in, through the door way. It kept seeping towards her from the corpse she knew was just outside the hut. The goddess of the ground didn't drink it up, so it welled up into a boiling lake, instead. The earth's thirst couldn't be quenched.

Outside, the newly widowed and orphaned poked their heads out of bloodied mud huts. Their eyes searched for hope. While still in the hut, Ana saw the souls of men leaving their bodies. They're taking hope with them for the journey to the afterlife. They're leaving but there would still be bodies rotting on the ground for days to come.

Ana counts, with her eyes closed, nodding her head in a particular rhythm, awaiting a sound all too familiar to her. And then...the first cry. Ana knew it was a woman who was too overwhelmed thinking about the hardship she is about to face, to think of the taboo of screaming over a corpse. Ana knew it was Udo. At this point, Udo did not care whether her screams attracted evil death spirits and made her children motherless as well as fatherless.

Udo was a bountiful woman. With arms that quaked when she gesticulated and a belly that spewed children like streams bled water. Everyone knew Udo was well taken care of, by her husband. The fact that her husband had no interest in baring any of the clan's respected titles was never an embarrassment to Udo, as long as she was fed well. Her happiness was anchored in her husband's barn being full of yam and that she could make pottage to pacify her herd of offspring. Udo lived up to her name: she was peaceful but coming between her and her comfortable life had once caused Udo to pour boiling water over her husband's mistress. She did not intend to show the gods any respect after taking away her livelihood. She didn't notice his chest still quivering.

Udo wailed and tugged at the dagger in her husband's neck. In her hysteria and lack of common sense she pulled the dagger across and slit his throat in one sweep, causing blood to gush out and his arm to jerk a little, but for the last time. Ana felt a shiver run down her spine. The gods were benevolent enough to give him one last moment with his wife, Udo; the one that brings peace.

Udo, startled at what had happened, knelt silently next to her husband's corpse and stared at him. In a trance; staring but not moving. Her husband bled onto the ground, but the gods did not drink this up, either. Soon Udo is engulfed by a puddle of her husband's blood. It crept around her and soaked the hands she had let fall at her sides. It wiggled into the gaps between her fingers and under her nails. The puddle surrounded her, and she sat in it with the most serene expression on her face as she stared at her husband. In a flash, Udo glided the dagger across her own throat without as much as a glance at her children, who looked on from her hut. It happened way too quickly for Ana to do anything but gasp. She growled at herself and gritted her teeth as she wished she didn't have these visions.

Udo's body collapsed across her husband's. The earth shook as the death spirits danced around her. Ana got another shiver that made her clutch her belly. The death spirits danced past the hut and Ana saw them through the walls as if they weren't there. They smile and mock at her as they dance over the body of him who owned her and dragged his spirit away. His soul wailed as he pleaded for Ana to save him, but she didn't know how to, so she just stood and watched as her insides churned.

The Beginning

When Ana first arrived in the valley, she was warmly received by the women. As she staggered into the road leading to the village square she was met by Akomah and Abadaye, who left their firewood at the side of the road to help her to the king's palace. They knew she needed help and figured the king would be best to decide what kind of help she would receive.

At the palace, there was a casual meeting in progress. It was between the king and a man that was built more like an animal than a human being. Even while arched over in thought, it was evident that he was oddly tall, and his limbs looked heavier than Ana herself. His matted hair made him look feral and he made Ana uncomfortable. It didn't help that he scolded the women, as soon as they entered the palace, for barging into a private meeting. The hunter was only appeased once the king saw Ana; battered and disheveled, and asked his friend to calm down. The king asked the women to explain themselves and they told him how they found Ana.

Ana noticed that the king's friend had a dagger in a sheath attached to his loin cloth and assumed he was a warrior – like the kind that had raided her village, killed her parents and left her for dead in the bush. She didn't remember much, except for the overwhelming pain of her people dying, which eventually made her pass out. Ana assumed the invaders threw her in the bush when they presumed her dead.

Ana winced as someone's touch jolted her out of her memory. The women had been told to take Ana to be cleaned. As they left, the man asked the king to excuse him, but the king insisted the man stay and help him decide Ana's fate. Though disinterested, the man stayed out of respect for his king.

Ana was returned and the king who explained that, while strangers were welcome on his land, they had very little agency unless married to a native. In such a case, Ana would become naturalized as part of his people, once she had a child. Alternatively, the king was also willing to accept her as a slave. She'd live in the wives' quarters and be fed every day. Ana thought about how much she just wanted to be home; to be surrounded by the life she was used to. Ana enquired whether she could stay under the king's guardianship until she found a man that would marry her. He calmly explained that women did not find husbands in his kingdom, should she choose to marry into his community, she would be married to the man she met in the palace earlier.

Ana contemplated choosing slavery in the king's palace. However, in the heat of the moment, she convinced herself that there is some autonomy in being a wife, even if there was probably no pride to be had. These people that have so kindly accepted her, do not seem to value women in the same way her people did. She thought that, in her own house, she might at least be able to rebuild her ancestors' shrine. She wasn't actually planning to have any children for the animal man but she was sure that her childlessness would be easier accepted by him than it would have been by the king. Ana's spirit knew that the king had enough domestic slaves and concubines and she'd rather be cursed than to become disposable. Her spirit also told her that the animal man had never been with a woman, which Ana found intriguing.

Ana was told that the man was a hunter and very rich. He was also a personal friend to the king and so the king was very keen to find him married. Although the king claimed that the hunter was glad to have finally been assigned a wife, he didn't look impressed. His displeased expression actually comforted Ana. If he was as uncomfortable with this union as she was, maybe he'd do well to just leave her alone. Maybe, he found women just as unappealing as Ana found men. Nonetheless, the marriage wasn't going to be an easy endeavor for Ana.

At first, she was glad for the help that the hunter had arranged for Ana. The village women passed by his house regularly and catered to Ana while he was out hunting. The name Obia got stuck after a while because she was still referred to as 'guest' despite her agreement with the king. She didn't really mind. She had people before she got to this village so where she happened to find herself had absolutely no bearing on her identity as a person. Ana couldn't care less what they called her.

The women would come and massage her with fragrant oils every day. During this time, her nurses were her only companionship as she was advised to stay indoors until fully recovered. Some spent hours admiring her tattoos while they were at it. Ana had the symbols of royalty and priesthood tattooed on her arms and chest. The women of this village obviously didn't know what they meant, but they were astonished at the fact that these drawings were permanent, and Ana didn't have to bother with chalk or charcoal every day. After a few days, all her bruises were healed, and she was allowed out. She was dressed in two pieces of bright cloth; one tied around her waist and the other went around her chest once, while the surplus was draped over her shoulder. She quite liked how she looked and for a short while, she felt good within herself. The only problem now, was that she had nothing to do.

There was no farm to plough or water to fetch. The hunter paid people for all those things. In the absence of anything to keep her busy, Ana decided to start building her shrine. She gathered large rocks to create the altar and thick tree branches to carve out the figurines representing the goddesses that were born before her. Once she had her things together, she searched her hut for one of the hunter's knives for carving. It was when she was barely done carving the first figurine that the hunter returned home to find her and her shrine in a corner of his compound.

She hadn't actually seen the hunter since the day they met, and he brought her to her new home. He had shown her everything around the hut and left with the instruction to wait for the village women that will do everything Ana required of them. So, when the hunter burst out into a frenzy, Ana was confused. She didn't think she was expected to go through the formalities of a wife welcoming the hunter, seeing that he had gone off without a word regarding where he was heading off to or how long he'd be. It wasn't until several moments into his ranting that Ana realized, his problem was with the shrine she was building. He chopped at the altar with his machete and cut her figurine into pieces before Ana could even utter a word of explanation. He shouted something about Ana trying to bewitch him and that he would kill her before she gets the chance to. The hunter went as far as raising his machete at Ana, but her aura suddenly burst into flames and he froze with his knife-wielding arm over his head. Ana just stood and stared at him with quiet resolve. Ana wasn't actually scared of dying. Even though she suddenly felt extremely hot with anger, she couldn't see her own aura. Ana was half expecting the hunter to bring his knife down on her head and she had no qualms about reuniting with her mother in the afterlife. Compelled by the energy Ana was subconsciously emitting, the hunter retreated into the hut like a wounded animal. Ana proceeded to rebuild her shrine and slept beside it that night.

Over the following months, the couple only conversed when the hunter was giving Ana instructions for preparing and curing the meat he brought home. He gave her the same instructions every time and when he got home he'd inspect her work. Then he'd leave the cooking area without another word. The food Ana cooked for him would always remain untouched. She assumed that he roasted the cured meats he takes to the bush and eats there but doesn't stop her from cooking enough for two people every day. It was more a matter of habit than obligation for Ana, so she ended up making good friends with the boy that brought the firewood in the mornings – he was the main beneficiary of Ana's cooking. She took great joy in seeing the boy enjoy her food. His people weren't so well off as hers had been and sometimes she even considered her current situation more privileged than his, so she was happy to have found a way to make him a little happy. After all, Ana had all the food and help she could ask for. Her mother and ancestors' spirits kept her company and the hunter hadn't touched her ever since she came to stay with him. Her life continued this way until she became a woman.

One night, Ana was in one of her deep sleeps that she is unable to wake up from until her dreams have reached their conclusion. Many a times she would wake up in a hot sweat, only to realize that she had slept well into the day. It gave others the impression that Ana was lazy but she knew that it is through those dreams that she knew when to make offerings to her shrine. Over time, her young friend and other people she had encountered, who happened to tell her their problems and be kind to her, found good fortune because Ana interceded for them appropriately. As time went on, Ana stopped feeling inadequate for not having a farm to tend to, like other women. Hers was an entirely different calling but it didn't really matter if nobody saw the work she did in the seclusion of her shrine.

In this particular dream, she saw her mother, surrounded by other women who looked eerily familiar, standing in a plunge pool at the bottom of a waterfall. The water and surrounding looked dark and gloomy and Ana at first assumed that they were trying to warn her about some danger. As the water poured over them, Ana traced it upwards. The cliff was so high that her view of the top was obscured by clouds. Eventually, Ana noticed that there were two magnificent legs hanging off the edge of the cliff and the water gushed from in between them. While Ana had seen many strange things in her dreams, she was taken aback by this enormous woman whose legs her almost as grand as the rock they hung from. When her mother called to her to enter the water, Ana was apprehensive, but she always obeyed her mother's instructions in her dreams. She had barely taken two strides into the water when the pool and the water flowing down from the goddess turned crimson. Ana didn't have a chance to panic before her entire environment transformed before her eyes. Sunlight appeared out of nowhere and brightened up the entire place. Suddenly, flowers and thick bushes bloomed up around the pool and fish gingerly swam around her feet, in the red tinted but glassy water. Ana's mother vaguely explains to her that "it's time" and Ana deduces that she is about to enter another phase of her life; both physically and spiritually.

When Ana woke up, she wasn't really surprised to feel an unfamiliar wetness when she touched herself. On examining her hand she found blood and was glad that her mother had taught her what the bleeding meant and how to deal with it. The hunter was no longer lying beside her so Ana knew that it was probably midmorning already, which might make the ritual she was going to perform a little difficult but she decided to do it anyway.

Ana got off the bed and gathered every piece of clothing and bedding that had been stained by her bleed. Naked, she walked out of her hut with the items in her arms, and towards her shrine where she burned everything. As expected, one or two villagers noticed Ana kneeling, naked, at her shrine and muttered amongst themselves about how Ana must be either mad or a witch. Once she was done, she went to bathe and intended to go about her day in the same way she did every day. It wasn't until she finished that Ana felt something that she had never felt before. She was expecting some discomfort, or pain even, but what she felt was more like a tingle. The sensation permeated from her neck, to her nipples and down to her clitoris. Inside, she could feel herself pulsating and it made sitting still impossible. Ana couldn't wait for her husband to return from hunting.

When the hunter returned that night, he was none the wiser that anything had changed. He trudged towards the hut as wearily as he did every evening. As he did on any other day, he slipped the game he had caught off his shoulder and was about to dump it in front of Ana, when he realized she isn't sitting outside as she usually did. When he checked the shrine and couldn't find her there, he just scuffed at the figurines and walked away. Ana never entered the hut until he was asleep, so he assumed she wasn't at home and went inside to find a unexpected sight. The hunter had never had any desire for Ana. Besides the fact that she was skinny and never smiled, she was an unwanted gift that had no appeal to him. Women generally didn't entice him and the fact that the villagers attributed his excellent hunting skills to his celibacy was all the more reason for him not consider sexual activity as a worthwhile endeavor. Yet, there was Ana who was acknowledging him for the first time since she came to live with him. She was not only looking him in the face but actually approaching him. When she put her arms around him and her head onto his chest in an affectionate embrace, the hunter could have sworn that this is how it felt to be inside his mother's belly. Ana placed his arms around her, and the hunter softened even deeper into her embrace.

After a while, Ana went ahead to slowly take off her husband's hunting gear. He watched her as she slipped his knife sheaths and pouches over his head. The fact that Ana had to tiptoe several times, didn't stop her. She then proceeded to untie his loin cloth. The hunter had never felt so vulnerable in the presence of a woman and he wasn't sure if it was ok for him to feel this way, but he felt too free to object. Ana guides him to sit on the bed while she unties her own clothes, all the while, staring her husband straight in the eyes. She had no apprehensions about what was about to occur, considering that she knew it was time. Once naked, Ana straddles her husband. As he enters her, she guides his lips to kiss her neck while they both let out soft moans. Her husband embraces her tightly as he dives deeper into her and simultaneously tries to suppress his desire to weep. Never would he have thought that being this close to a woman would feel this freeing. His face is still buried in Ana's neck when she pushes him to lie back and glides his hands up her thigh, then her waist and up to her breasts. The hunter cups her breasts as she folds over to place one in his mouth and cradle his head as he gently sucks on her nipple. The hunter moans loudly when she leans back again, letting him slide into her fully. Ana sits and caresses her husband's chest for a while, occasionally kissing his shoulders, neck and face. She runs her fingers through his beard and hair while softly imitating the waist movements of the dances her mother taught her as a child, all the while keeping to the tempo of spirit drums playing within her. The faster the drums, the faster Ana would move her waist. Her husband's moans cheered her on and she watched his face squeeze up into a painful pleasure, but she wouldn't stop even when the feeling threatened to overwhelm him. He moaned her name louder and she moved faster until Ana felt her climax surge through her body and her husband shot off his back with a deep roar to cling to her as he also climaxed.

The two stayed entwined for a while and Ana could feel her husband's fluids and her blood leak out of her. When her husband finally let go, Ana got up, took a shower and went ahead to cure the game he had brought home. She waited until she was sure he was going to be asleep before she joined him.

While not much changed about Ana's relationship with the hunter, they did continue to sleep with each other whenever Ana felt like it. The hunter had no objections against appeasing her insatiable hunger, but Ana was concerned and when she started feeling different, she knew the worst had happened. Suddenly, Ana would have visions of her mother when she was awake, and she could anticipate things before they happened more acutely. She could hear the thoughts of others and see through inanimate objects. When she noticed her own aura and was able to see that of others, it occurred to her that something strange must be happening.

When she dreamt of fish one night, she woke up to tell the hunter that she was pregnant. He was neither impressed nor disappointed but told her that he would tell the doula at the king's palace to check on her every once in a while. Once he had left for the bush, Ana considered whether she wanted to keep this child, but her mother made her to understand that it was an honor to birth the next priestess of the goddesses. Ana decided that her mother was right – she hoped that having this child would add purpose to her life in the same way her mother's life was dedicated to raising her. Ana missed her mother more than ever. Ana wished that the new king had never disrespected her mother, nullifying her protection over the land. More so, she wished that her mother hadn't tried to defend her people against the gods.

As time went on, Ana became tired of the gifts that came with the child she was carrying. Being able to hear people's thoughts was especially exhausting because it forced Ana to face a reality that she was never really concerned with. She had never cared much about how the villagers felt about her and since they didn't say anything to her face, for fear of the hunter, it had never occurred to her that they disliked her. Yet, suddenly, she could hear the lady that brought her fruit call her a witch. Another wondered whether Ana was mad or whether her the offerings she made in the nude were to keep the hunter docile. Ana knew she had no reason to force the hunter to stay married to her but the fact that people thought she would bewitch him, hurt her feelings. Ana still handled her interactions with grace until one day when the firewood boy came to drop off a delivery. A couple of times Ana had caught him thinking of undressing her but Ana pegged it down to childish exuberance. She knew that his social status probably didn't get him much interaction with girls so she let him have his fantasies until they became very frequent. When she confronted him about it, the boy pounced on her and attempted to rape her.

He was able to overpower Ana who was always tired nowadays and was just about to insert himself into her when a force form within Ana surged through the boy and he fell to the ground; dead.

It wasn't long before some villagers came to enquire about the commotion and found the boy lying lifeless on the ground. Their immediate instinct was to arrest Ana and take her to the palace where the king judged against her. As a stranger to his land, she was always going to lose. She felt no inclination to announce that she was pregnant. Ana was tired of being alone and misunderstood. She was ready to submit to whatever punishment the king was going to sentence her to – preferably death. Her hearing was barely about to be concluded when war horns could be heard in the palace and panic broke out. The horns were foreign and a sign of an attack.

Letting Go

Now, months later, Ana was watching the same spirits that turned on her mother carry away the hunter's soul as he begged for her help. During their time together, he never acknowledged her divinity yet suddenly she was supposed to conjure the power to defend him but she didn't know how.

Tears ran down her face as the pain of guilt hurt her heart. Once she had made it back to her hut, it was the hunter that tried to defend her. All night she could see him cut down one foreign warrior after the other. It wasn't until daybreak that one of them blinded the hunter with an amulet that another was able to stick a sword in his stomach. Nobody came inside the hut. The hunter was obviously wealthy considering the size of his hut and the pelts he wore but not one warrior came inside to look for loot. They had come solely for blood. Ana watched the blood that was still pooling in the middle of the room and went to touch it. It was still warm. Her daughter kicked more aggressively the further Ana submerged her hand into the blood. She wasn't sure what would happen, so she prayed to her mother as she slowly let herself fall into, and be submerged in the blood of an innocent man that fought for her.

JUJU LOVE

Thirty-six hours since I last saw you
But there's still a quiver in my knickers that makes
me suddenly know how to dance
Veiled in white, but with every shimmy my
innocence slips off my skin
I come to you in all the full dignity of nakedness
Body dipped in potions of shea and cocoa
Curves resembling the bends in the river that life
springs from
And I'm waiting for your fountain to well up inside
me

I don't know how you got a hold on me, but your
magic is evident
I couldn't find the calabash with the red handkerchief
inside
But the red in your eyes, as you stared me down,
broke the dam holding back my ocean
My inner Oshun bursts out into light
And there's an explosion that all the ancestors
applaud

I was loveless until your juju filled me
Until you satiated my hunger for the divine – one
tongue lashing at a time

Now I'm sick in the morning as my desire grows for
you and takes over my senses
The smell of food is unappealing 'cause now ... *e be
only you I wan eat.*

BEFORE BEES AND FLOWERS

You're beautiful.
Not because you're black but because you're a human being

Because every single second, a circus of miracles happen in your body to make it work

Imagine the orchestra of percussion that is your beating heart
that's art in itself

But being black means that your skin is rich with melanin
Maybe less than some but definitely more than others
Your hair will grow from your scalp coily and upwards like Ivy
Your nose will probably be broad, your forehead high and your lips thick

You will have to be strong and resilient
Think twice before you speak, so your words can have twice the impact to be acknowledged once
You will be outspoken because you can't suffer in silence for the sake of it
You will be proud - because it's necessary for survival.

So let no one tell you otherwise because I've told you why YOU'RE BEAUTIFUL.

A LIFE IN BRIEF

Since I never got the chance to read you bed time stories, how about I tell you a story now. Ten years ago, when I met you, you were nothing but a shape on a screen but I was so awestruck. The internet told me you were only about the size of an avocado but the concept of you being inside me, in the first place, seemed so abstract. How did I deserve someone so beautiful? The very moment I heard your heartbeat, I also heard all aspects of my life fall into their respective harmonies. My rhythm had changed – your presence was my heart song.

I was going to give it all up for you. Babies and degrees – in that order. Nothing else mattered and if you had stayed a little longer I could have taught you so many things. Like the fact that A stands for Accra; the city that has my heart. Where Z still stands for zebra; a kind of crossing nobody acknowledges.

On the other hand, I may have also taught you that as a woman, you have to make do with what men throw at you. I probably would have glorified my struggle, while alienating you. God forbid that I ever hang my sacrifices over you head but I was very foolish then and you deserved better. I would have never known the things I now know about my body, if you had stayed. I have read so much because I wanted to understand why you left. You didn't go because you were unloved but I guess my heart was a healthier place to grow in.

My body wasn't good enough and that's ok. Maybe I should have prayed more to annul the fact that you were a product of fornication. I never asked for forgiveness for making you but I'm sorry that your father didn't want you. You deserved a mother who doesn't settle for a man whose heart is with someone else just because his arms are familiar.

I understand why you would rather die than be my daughter – I can empathise – but it hurts that you died inside me. It hurts that my body was more coffin than cocoon for you – that my love smothered, rather than soothed you. Maybe I crowned you too early for your little head to manage. Being my everything is a burden I regret putting on you – it is unjustifiable and I'm sorry but I won't apologize for holding on to your memory for all these years. Often, the flashback of the flutters in my abdomen give me hope that maybe you'll send me another child. They won't be you, and I know that my mind has rationalised my barrenness, but sometimes I see what you would have looked like and I miss the idea of you.

It's been ten years since you died, Serwah, and only now do I love myself enough to have been able to love you like a mother should, and part of that is because you didn't stay for me to love you. I have to thank you for that.

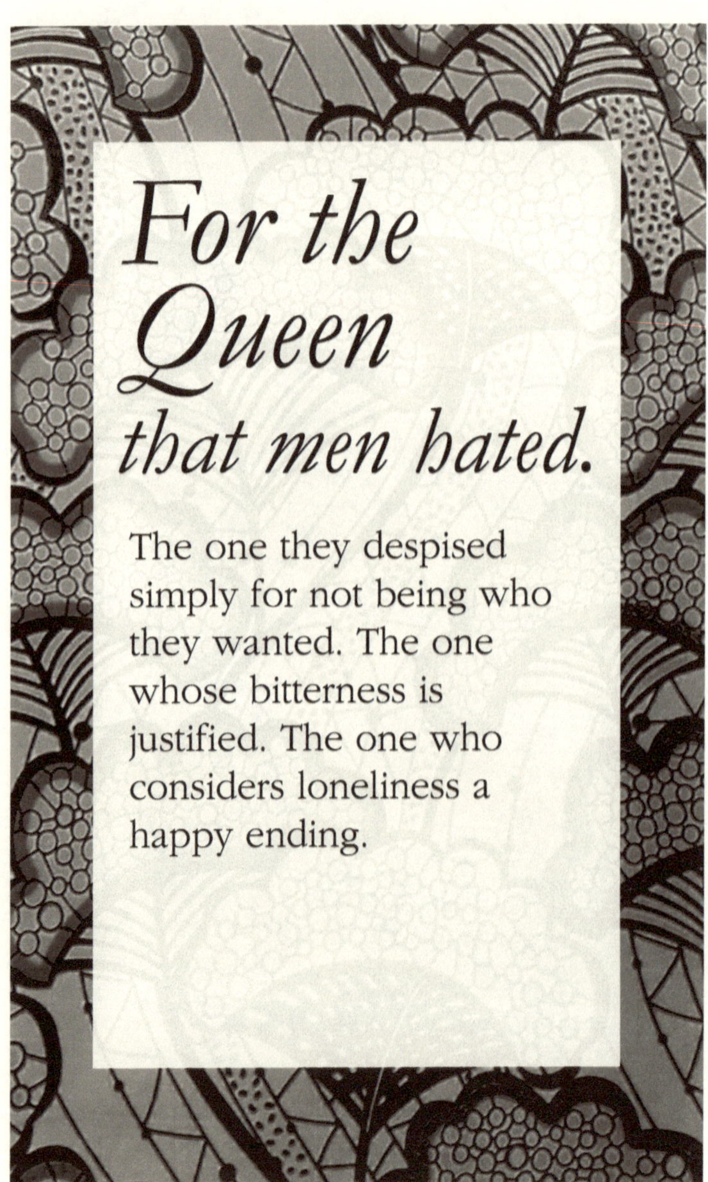

For the
Queen
that men hated.

The one they despised
simply for not being who
they wanted. The one
whose bitterness is
justified. The one who
considers loneliness a
happy ending.

LIMBO

There's a place called limbo

Here you'd never say you love me but you'd also
never cheat
Because you take my feelings to heart
Even if those feelings don't go beyond me buying
you a card for your birthday

Our boundaries are buoys in the ocean that help us
avoid disaster
But we're not going anywhere
It's all shallow enough for me to stay grounded

While I'd love to love you, common sense won't let
me
My obsession with peace is our demise
Even though I miss the fight I have to put up to curb
my smile
every time I hear you explain guitar riffs to me
You and I could have been sweet in the in-between

I'm trying to get to heaven
making love to someone that's in love with someone
else won't get me there

The bar is too low to go under
You haven't blown my back out enough for me to
bend that way
so I'll just rise above and be off

I'd rather burn with Hades getting over you
Than stay in god-forsaken limbo

THIS AIN'T IT

So, this is not my life

I'm not supposed to be the
closer-to-thirty-than-twenty spinster I pitied as a child
The auntie whose integrity I questioned for being
single past twenty-five is now me
My heart shouldn't be numb to this fact
Or to affection
the idea of sleeping next to someone I have feelings
for, shouldn't create so much tension

Nonetheless, I find myself satisfied with half of a
heart because I only have a little of mine to give
And the thought of marrying someone, in the way
God intended it, gives me hives
I'm the woman that has been alone so much that she
cannot fathom tolerating love
I've become my mother – go figure.

I wasn't supposed to be childless
They declared, by holy passages, that I'm not barren
Yet here I am, nursing the memory of the child I
almost had nine years ago
Cutting off friendships with women who I can no
longer relate to, because I have had to curb my
enthusiasm for children
Other people's babies make me almost as sick as my
uterus does

I shouldn't be writing poetry

I shouldn't be at a point where I spend so much of
my time in fear

that I spend none fulfilling my purpose
Anxiety attacks aren't my portion
Yet here I am, wide awake
Considering everything that could go wrong when
having to interact with white people

This is not my life because it's not what I planned it
to be.
It's not what the preachers told me when they were
in the spirit
 I messed up a little bit but got my shit together and
sacrificed all my financial freedom for an education
Wasn't that enough reparation?

I am too beautiful and too smart for this life.
I am a good, loving, talented person.
This shouldn't be the life of someone that makes
kelewele as good as mine.

This is not my life because my mother didn't leave
her home for a foreign land for this
Jesus died so I can have better but here I am…
A heathen, waiting to die.

HAPPY ENDINGS

It's been a good run
Race to the finish line
It's been a challenge, one I couldn't decline
I love the chase just as much as he does

He taught me that I can be selfless
I can love unconditionally
Helplessly; content with just him
One thousand six hundred and forty days of my life
I shared my heart with him
For four hundred and twenty five It was all fun and
games
But my cardiovascular muscles skipped a beat
as we first kissed
They had to stay still while fate inked his name on
one of my ventricles
For four and a half years it stayed there

When my heart gave up on me my mind stayed loyal
to him
Always remembering spending his birthday together
Remembering sitting on my porch
bonding over past mistakes like something out of a
movie
Reiterating what's now poetry
I recall pouring out my secrets similar to how the
heavens
showered blessings onto us

My tears watered the seed of our love
It grew bigger than my dreams
It grew heavy on my wings
They grew heavy

If it meant this much it must have been real, right?
I remember the feel of your heart beating against
mine
No clothes barring us
Admitting everything, showing our scars
As you looked into me
you looked right through me
In the streets my substance is abundant
but in the confines of our passion
I became transparent
Vulnerable to your X-ray vision
I allowed you know me to precision
I recollect being in your arms
They engulf me as you tower over me like the great
rock I'd hoped for you to be
Those arms were warm, caring
Temporarily
You play with my hair like they're the strings holding
my soul together
Teasing it into a tousled mess

My emotions follow

My mind races

Things I thought I'd never say or do
I did for you
Love does those things and I'm glad to have been her
slave
If anyone asks I can gloriously say
I loved you all the way
I couldn't have loved you any better
I couldn't have loved you anymore
The number of stars in the sky were minute
The words to describe it eludes me

For a while I made your happiness priority over my
existence
Retained persistence even when your support wasn't
evident
supported your ambition
Made them my mission
I was the epitome of devotion
To your well being
I adored you for the words you spoke
accepted you for the ones you didn't
Addressed you with all the respect
known to my feeble mind
But that isn't enough apparently and that's ok

The earth will continue to rotate
But we've come to an end
Now that these tears have fallen I'll never shed
another
Now that these words are written there won't be
sequels to the poems you can call yours
I'm free to dream again

I'm free to imagine reciprocity
To have a conscience clear of your guilt
I've lost you and I'm happy
Contentment is a great gift

I'll always love the chase but being IN love with him
is a burden I can no longer lift

I drop the hurt and the confusion
It's hard but that's my retribution
I loved harder than my mind could comprehend
I loved the chase longer than my legs could carry it
to end
It's gone further than what either of us could mend
So I'm breaking it
I'm letting it all spill and then I'll move on with the
current

The chase is over
I made it to the finish line

I'm worn
I'm tired

I'm gasping for air to fill my lungs and pump up my
chest again
But at the end I came out whole
I climb back on my throne
And worship myself again

My nights will be peaceful
My days amazing
I'm leaving wiser and more graceful
And never returning

BROWNIES

Dennis Kowa hated hospitals. To him, they meant death and Dennis was never wrong.

Emilie Kyle was a beautiful woman. her skin was tanned a particular shade of brown that resembled molasses and had the same sheen. Her facial features were slender and soft. Emilie had the sort of style that couldn't be pinpointed. She always wore her hair straight, parted in the middle, without layers and down to her waist. when she completed a task at her desk, she would swoop the hair behind her shoulder in a smooth motion, exposing the tattoo of the number eleven on her neck which contrasts with the conservative skirt suits she wore. They were usually grey or navy blue, only made a little exciting by the same pair of red pumps she wore every day. The shoes made her exceptionally tall. Though very slim, she always looked quite assertive when craned over the boundary of an associate's cubicle, politely urging them to provide information Kowa had requested. Emilie rarely smiled and walked the corridors of Kowa, Hills and Cain without a swing in her step, yet everyone admired her as she slid along groggily. Despite her demeanour, Emilie was too beautiful not to look at.

Emilie was top of her class at law school and just happened to have a strong affinity towards the theories of Freud. Yet, neither those things or any other superficial part of her life explains why she was a legal secretary as opposed to a high-flying attorney. In her defence, she is not just any receptionist, but guards the entrance to the 'devils lair'. Emelie's boss, Dennis Kowa – an odd character in many ways – was never a man of leisure. As a matter of fact, he had put a lot of life's pleasures on hold to put all his efforts into making his career. He married young to get it out of the way but had no children.

It was 11 am when Dennis jumped into the luxury car that he adored. In the car, he fastened the last button on his shirt and put on a tie that he pulled out of his glove compartment. The rest of his impeccable ensemble would be worn in the parking lot at the office. He turned to pass his hand over the new suit jacket hanging in the back of his car and smiles to himself. Recently, nothing made him happier than the frivolity of premium quality hand-woven textiles. A short drive, a few blocks from his previous location, Dennis pulled into a garage and parked in his allocated parking spot. He finished off his look before heading upstairs. Dennis pulled a long blonde hair from the fabric of his trousers just as he is about to leave the elevator, smiles and then proceeds towards his office as he discards it carelessly.

For the past seven months, Emilie's boss walked into the office at 11.30am on the dot – only on Tuesdays. On any other day of the week Mr Kowa is in the office at 7.30am. Of course, nobody is that meticulously late every single week, on the same day of the week, but Emilie doesn't ask questions. Emilie was Kowa's receptionist exactly because she doesn't ask questions. She owed her freedom to him and knows that questions can lead to a lot of trouble. Emilie also makes a great substitute for Dennis when he is not around so he is barely missed.

"Any messages for me?" Dennis asks as he paces past Emilie.

"No." She replies, without looking up from her computer.

As he walks past, he pats Emilie softly on the shoulder in a fatherly manner, which makes her turn her head towards him slightly, in acknowledgement. Dennis is in his office when Emilie calls towards him.

"Oh actually, there's a message on the answering machine."

Dennis is inside his office, pouring himself a coffee and taking a bite out of a muffin from a basket filled with them. The basket also has a note with a heart on it.

"I haven't had a chance to check it yet but since you're here..."

Emilie didn't like to lie but she also didn't want to listen to another message that would probably be Dennis' wife frantically sobbing, trying to find out where he is. The message wasn't there when they both left very late last night so it had to have been left even later or very early this morning.

"It's fine. I'll..." the phone rings, interrupting him briefly.

"I got it."

Dennis picked up the phone and settled into his chair, leaning back into it. Suddenly, as he listened to what the other person had to say, he props himself back up. Emilie looked on through the glass walls of Dennis' office as the colour drains from his face. She wasn't sure how karma was coming, but it was here and it didn't care that Dennis didn't like hospitals.

The last time Dennis was in a hospital, he watched his parents die. He didn't care much about his dad getting into a freak accident at work, but his mother getting a stroke the same week felt like the entire universe was against him. That is when he met Emilie.

On one of the days he came to see his mother, he saw a young girl sitting in the waiting room praying. Although she did it under her breath, Dennis could hear her asking God to make sure that the bullet she'd put in her boyfriend's bowel wouldn't kill him. She also prayed that the police wouldn't find the drug money in her apartment and promised she'd concentrate on school if God delivered her. While

Dennis thought her praying such a prayer out loud was careless, he felt inclined to speak to Emilie and see how he could help. He knew from experience that some men deserved to be shot dead.

Three months later Dennis' mum died. His dad followed shortly after, but Dennis never set foot in a hospital again. Now, he had to, because his wife had been in an accident. He hadn't thought he cared enough before, but he caught himself praying that God should save her. Dennis told God he was sorry and that he promised to love her better, but it was too late. After sitting around in agonizing anticipation, the doctors came to tell him there was nothing they could do.

Back in the office, Emilie stared at the red blinking light on the answering machine. She knew she should listen. Whatever was in that message was important and when Dennis came back from wherever he had rushed off to, so frantically, he'd want to know.

Dennis got into his car and drove straight home. Everything moved in slow motion. He imagined this was hell, and the distortions in his vision were heat waves instead of tears.

Emilie played the message.

"Dennis, it's Anna. I haven't seen you since yesterday and I have found out why I don't see you for a day or two every week. I just wanted to say it's ok, I've come to peace with it."

There's a long pause and Emilie considers stopping the playback but then Anna continues.

"Do you remember the first day we met? It was my parent's house. You were so skinny and when I saw you, through the blinds in my bedroom, I gave my sisters a disappointed look."

Anna chuckles.

"I thought you were going to be this tall, immaculately dressed lawyer that was suave and smooth, but you were just you; shy and quiet and skinny – in ugly corduroy trousers. I didn't think I'd like you. I was ready to tell my parents I didn't like you but then I heard you speak about your work, and how badly you wanted to become partner at a renowned firm and I found that very sweet. I had started eating the brownies you know - the brownies I made for you? My sister asked her friend, Tilly, whose brother went to college with you about you. He mentioned you love brownies so I made them but I almost ate them all. I almost didn't love you but then I did, even though I'm not sure if you ever did."

Anna sighs deeply.

"I know about the other woman so I'm leaving. I would stay, I have stayed even through all the changes you've gone through, but I was making brownies today and I realised; I don't think I can love you anymore. Goodbye Dennis."

Dennis staggered into the front door; through the living room and into the kitchen before slumping on a chair. On the dining table sat a tray of brownies and Anna's wedding band.

HAVISHAM EFFECT

Miss Havisham
Nothing without you
I'm the ghost of a bride
And the ghost of good virtue
I'm empty
There but not quite
I'm the air that's required
For you to live
But you don't need me

You're just as much a ghost as I've been
Something I like to imagine
A fabrication of my non-existing mind
The one I lost
No the one I placed in a box along with my heart
On which I placed your address, underneath the
stamp
I licked it, so you could have some of my DNA
And understand what I'm made of
The desire to be yours

So I set myself ablaze
I burn this girl so she can rest with you in hell
Where you'll be going
Whilst I rejuvenate myself
Make like a phoenix and rebirth all of my cells
Without the membranes that imprisoned my true self
So I stand by as the rising smoke twirls that river of
white into the air

Swallowing it up
And then suddenly its done

Miss Havisham is dead
And I am free to run

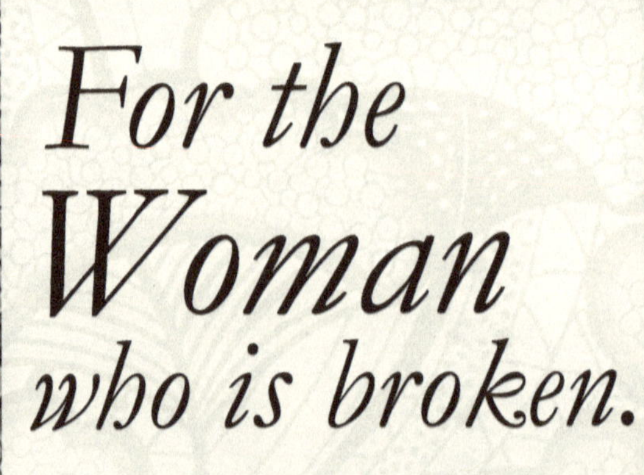

For the Woman who is broken.

Whose future has only reflected her past and doesn't believe in the light at the end of the tunnel. She knows her love doesn't change the world, but she does it anyway – with the slithers that are left of her heart.

WISE WORDS

I come from a place where elders don't lie so I always believed that taking hot showers accelerated aging

I dabbed lotion on my bosom for most of my life because massaging would make my breasts too big Elders don't lie so I was certain that, if I didn't throw my last milk tooth onto our roof, I'd never have a perfect set of pearly whites

Since the genesis of my amalgamation into scholarly environs I had it ingrained in my cognitive thinking that big words made you smarter

I ate twice my usual intake of fish during exam season, so that I'd shark through without revising
I never took biscuits from strangers in fear they'd turn to limbs in my pocket or money from the ground to avoid being a victim of ritualists

I am from a place where elders never lie so as he put his hand over my mouth to quieten my whimper and pulled aside the thong I shouldn't have worn, under the skirt that didn't reach my knees, I thought of what elders had told me would happen to girls that went to see boys after dark

And that day I knew it was true, because elders never lie.

HAPPY MEAL

Wide awake, yet utterly removed from reality I soaked in the sensation of my body sinking deeper into the soft mattress. The duvet was thrown over me shabbily, so my nipples hardened at the breeze in the room, yet I felt hot inside. My blood was boiling, and I could hear my pulse in my own ears but you could never tell from my blank expression. I must have looked beautiful, ethereal even, with the mild sunset rays creeping through the blinds and trickling over my limp body.

It's interesting how the light always breaks into evil, even if you take extra measures to make sure neighbors can't witness the struggle from their parallel windows. Every sweet word he whispered and every spontaneous appearance on my route to or from school had been a pin in his plot. In my already malfunctioning mind, however, he seemed totally legit. I wondered if he felt as bad as I did.

I stirred, and pain shot through my body, while my thigh cramped up. There wasn't a firm hand restraining my cries this time. Looking up and seeing his figure in the door way, with his finger to his lips made me angry. It was his fault I was in pain in the first place but more so mine so the next time I attempted to move I clasped my mouth hard and jolted into a standing position. I almost tipped over but the hard edge of the desk caught me. I wished I had been able to fall asleep after he slumped down beside me and never woken up.

Getting dressed was a challenge with just one opposable thumb – the other had been twisted into disfunction. My neck had bruises on them that would suggest a passionate encounter and my labia was dripping as though I was expecting some pleasure, but it was really just a notice that I should have booked my first HIV test. I ignored all of that and made for the door. He offered to walk me home and I was in no position to object.

We approached a McDonalds en route. Me, walking in shameful silence and he, going on about something trivial I had no cognitive capability to make note of. At that point, I felt like the only thing that could loosen the knot in my throat was all the hydrogenated fats in the world, so I asked him if we could get food. He ordered me a happy meal and the server asked if I wanted a toy. A question I will never forget. Somebody acknowledged my childhood – or at least it felt like it. I wanted to say yes as my heart warmed a little, at the memories of when I'd see my mother on the weekend and she'd bring me happy meal toys from work. I wanted to settle into the idea that I was still young and I had time to fix my life. He snapped at the server with a sharp 'no' and I snapped back into the reality that he was the one buying. A barter trade secured with food and affection I should have received from anywhere else but from a rapist. About two streets from mine he stopped. Usually, I'd beg him to take me to the front door. He'd decline and I'd thank him for walking me that far. This time, I kept walking absentmindedly until he pulled me back by the wrist and wrapped his arms around me, with my wrist still shackled in his hands. He was strong for a smallish man but not strong enough to justify the bruises I had let him give me. I'm embarrassed at the inhibitions I have let him give me. Cuddles feel violent ever since I learnt that they were a Trojan horse.

I kissed him dutifully and he told me I was beautiful. I smiled a genuine smile. As soon as I walk into my home, I'd be reminded that fat girls have no business eating fast food so I loved that he would lie to me like this. I loosened one hand from his grip and caressed his face. I probably loved this man as much as he made me want to kill myself. I kissed him softly and he tightened his embrace as his hand slipped down to my butt. I could feel myself lubricate – just like it did the night before. I was testing myself and the conclusion was that this body was his. Many times, in the future, he'd tell me no one can get me as wet as he can and somehow that meant something to me. Too bad sex ed didn't teach us how good the vagina is at self-preservation in event of trauma.

We finally said our good-byes and I could feel him watching me as I walked towards my front door. I didn't look back. It was enough for one evening. Once inside, I took off my black shoes and slipped my rucksack off my back. Before entering the living room, I made sure to tuck in the stray braids that had escaped my pony tail. I greeted my aunt with a wry 'good evening' as she watched me walk past with her mouth turned down and her eyes sizing me up. I didn't have to look at her to know she was doing it. She had always accused me of staying out late to get fucked by useless boys so that day was just a self-fulfilling prophesy.

'Where's Rita's McDonald's?' she says as I was almost over the threshold to the kitchen. I look at the food bag in my hand and decide it's not worth it so I turn around and drop it on the coffee table without a word.

In the kitchen, I peeled off my purple jumper and slipped my tie over my head. I needed a bottle of water to take to my room because I wasn't planning on leaving my room that night. I also had a piece of cake in my bag that I brought home for my aunt so I put that in the fridge as I took out the water. As I trudged up the stairs, I saw my little cousin at the top of the stair case so I sighed and let out a little prayer. I didn't want to deal with her. I was tired and in pain and I couldn't deal with a slap from my uncle that evening. Strangely, my cousin just stood there, smiling, as I approached. When I was at the top, she gave me an envelope and then squeezed past me, heading downstairs.

Inside my room, I sat on my bed slowly because my groin still hurt. After I took off the rest of my school uniform I opened the envelope. There was a handmade card inside. On the front, there were flowers and a smiling sun; all drawn in crayon. I stared at the sun for a while, I wondered about how naive it is for children to draw a smiling sun when really, I can only imagine it grieves at the things it witnesses every day. The sun must be tired of rising every day, only to find that humans just get trashier, every morning.

I opened the card eventually and was finally able to cry. The knot dissolved into sobs that I had to suppress but were necessary. 'Happy Fourteenth Birthday' will forever be the most bittersweet birthday message I have ever received.

DILEMMA

If only you could hear me

I dare you to let me leave
let my hands work swiftly
With a blade across my arm
I'm drifting

Nope, not gone yet
Don't worry, devil, my untimely death can wait a sec
Holding out on God, who'd promised me I'd rest
But I guess, we have our definitions messed up

Life has a way of making you give up on it - on
dreams
But sometimes it leaves hunger for just one thing

When everything is melting together in frustration
you can often find a love for something trivial
Keeping you from slicing lengthwise this time

Giving you hope that you might bare fruit
because of your budding talent.
You want so bad to show the world why you're here

Unfortunately, you also want your demons silenced
I get it, but all I hear is sirens.

OF COLOURED GIRLS

I keep telling myself that if my daughter(s) went
through any of the things I went through
All hell would break loose

I'm sure my mother thought the same

I want to say that I'd rather die than watch my child
be raped
But who would wash the bloody sheets once she
manages to crawl out of them?

I have no choice but to be there
Because statistically my daughters will be as unlucky
as I was

But let the difference be open mouths and minds
I pray that they trust me enough to protect them

That they'll tell me about a man's transgressions
Even if that man shares my bed

May they never try to spare my head

Maybe I should just raise boys
Teach them not to rape

I say this as though they are safe

MATTER OVER MIND

Even after we repainted her room to make it less gloomy, Sarah still finds it hard to get out of bed despite the bright midmorning sun. To be fair, we actually changed the room to make it as white as possible to emphasize blood stains. Sarah's favourite colour is black but I'm sure that's just because of her moods.

I usually come and help her out of bed but as I walk into her room I find her hoisting herself up with the aid of the railing attached to her bed. Her gnarly fingers wrap themselves around the bar and I can see she's getting more exhausted with every movement. She can't have been awake for more than an hour – because that's when I checked on her – but she's already weak again. She flinches when I try to help her, but I'm used to the back and forth at this point. She no longer talks or screams and she's too frail to fight my help so, eventually, she just gives up and I link my arm with hers to support her. Sometimes, I forget how emaciated she has become, until I can practically feel her skin slip against her bones. You would have never thought that she was a chubby baby.

Once we're out in the corridor, just a few steps past the threshold of her room, Sarah often stops to stare at herself in the family pictures on the commode. She was a healthy weight in most of them and the psychiatrist suggested we keep them there to remind her that she was happier when she was healthy. Sarah is indeed smiling in the pictures but I'm not sure anymore if she was happy then.

Going down the stairs, Sarah likes to lean on the wall rather than put her weight on me. As she is usually just wearing fuzzy socks, Sarah slips along on the polished wood stairs and sometimes it makes me smile because it reminds me of her and her sister 'skating' down the stairs. That's how Lynn broke two of her teeth and had to have them fixed in the emergency room. To this day, Lynn herself insists we should have let her grow up with two broken front teeth; that it would have given her 'character'. There was no way I was going to let any of my children look like savages, but I have grown to appreciate her lack of vanity. Maybe, if Sarah was more like her sister…. The staff have learnt to scurry by, at our arrival downstairs, or focus on something else because Sarah doesn't like being stared at – the irony. When she is out of sight, everything revolves around her, anyway. She's the reason the floors are kept heated until way into the summer.

Meal times are difficult, but they have become easier since we've been more vigilant about Sarah's self-harming. Occasionally, we'd find a cut, or a pierce wound on her hip while she slept, and we'd have to sweep everywhere she has access to, for contraband objects. The only way she gets to appease her urge to inflict pain on herself is by practically pouring piping hot food down her throat.

At first, I made sure that her food was always served at room temperature, but she wouldn't eat it. She became thinner and thinner. No matter how much I screamed at her through my tears, she would only stare at me blankly until I gave up and retreated with a headache. Eventually I gave up, I let her hurt herself in the hopes that it'll help in the long run. Every meal comes with the promise of a hot cup of tea after. This works most times but more recently, I've caught her making herself vomit after meals.

Occasionally, I have caught Sarah standing in front of her bathroom mirror, admiring her body. She'd strip naked and smile to herself. It is the most disturbing thing to watch. She is so skinny she can barely stand, yet, there she is, happy at the way she looks. Her face is gaunt, her ribs are protruding so much, and her pelvic bones look like they're just draped with skin.

Ordinarily, dealing with Sarah's anorexia and depression would be easier if it wasn't my fault. Sarah stopped eating the day she found out her father had raped her sister. One summer, Lynn had come back from boarding school after staying away for a whole year. On her arrival from the airport, we were all astonished at how much she had grown. My lanky, awkward pre-teen had suddenly broadened out and gained some curves. Her breasts had come in and she even had hips. We all thought Lynn would never find a husband, as skinny as she was. Sarah was the curvy one.

One night, I walked into my daughter's room and found my husband on top of my daughter. In court, I heard my other daughter testify about how he had been sexually assaulting her for years. I was delirious with confusion through it all but it was Lynn that really lost her mind. When my husband was acquitted, she walked into traffic, just as we left the courthouse. Sarah didn't eat for weeks after that day and then we had to force feed her. Every time I begged her to eat she'd tell me it's the only way my husband won't come back to find her. We haven't seen him since the day of his verdict and have moved houses, but she is sure he'd be back. He always did say that no matter where we were in this world, he'd always come for us. I have a bullet ready for that day.

For the
Crazy
Cat Lady.

Her mind wanders and
she is barely coherent
anymore, but she is still
human. She is still pas-
sionate and when she
dies, there'll be stories told
about her.

REM

"Hello, my name is Annabel and ..."

Unfortunately, I didn't quite catch the end of what she was saying. My mind was still swaying between realms and I couldn't quite concentrate because I couldn't figure out where I was. I could vaguely perceive the applause at the end of her address, though.

 I could hear the midnight brigade of police cars, with deafening sirens, blast past my bedroom window. My skin crawled with the same irritation it always does, when they zoom past my bedroom window, even though I wasn't actually in my bedroom. I wince with contempt as I try to reposition myself under my covers and metal springs prick my sides.

I must have winced a little too loud. The castigation from myself to myself – for not ordering that memory foam mattress off the shopping channel two days ago – was interrupted by a sudden silence in the room. Everyone was facing me, and I wasn't quite sure why I wasn't freaking out at the faces staring at me with disapproval. My wince was definitely too loud.

Not that it did anything to help me figure out where I was, but suddenly realised I was surrounded by about two dozen of what seemed to be a pic'n'mix bag of ogres and trolls. I wished my boyfriend was there. My lack of mythical creature knowledge is, indeed, a useful trait. I would have had a heart attack if my subconscious was able to imagine whatever the hell David said a Blemmyes is.

The Ogre's for one, fit my schemas to the T. Too tall, too bulky in all the wrong places and I couldn't tell their genders apart. Then again, why was that important anyway? The trolls were the more interesting creatures. There were tall and slender ones, shorter ones with nicely cropped hair in plaid shirts and khaki shorts; hipster trolls that moved into Hackney with the delusion that they wouldn't have to step in a black kid's blood to get their pint of kale juice.

I wondered whether it was still January. I wasn't cold, but I could feel a breeze from somewhere. It didn't make sense until I turned around and realised the back of the room was open to the universe. Not in a classroom mood board kind of way but actual star clusters and nebulas. As my heart dropped at the sight of planets floating by at arm's length, I swore I'd never Astrophysics and Chill again. I also realised that these creatures were still staring at me while I took forever to get my bearings, so I needed to snap out of it.

'I'm so sorry, please continue.' I wail, throwing my hands up and then clasping them together on top of my lips, partly to demonstrate my intent to be a silent observer from then on and also because I was reciting Sunday's scripture in my head. You know, in case this was it.

As everybody turns around to face the podium again, I hear the tower clock at the corner of my street strike 4am. I have two hours before I need to be up for work so whatever I was doing here, I need to do it quick. Too bad I had no clue what that was. As I contemplated what to do, I see someone take Annabel's place at the front.

I fixed my focus completely on this young gentleman, who seemed oddly human. He had the clearest blue eyes – see-through almost. He looks at me and holds my gaze for a minute and I'm not sure why he would be interested in me, after I had made myself such a fool.

'Hi, I'm Donald.' He says averting his gaze from mine and looking straight ahead into the beautiful arrangement of milkyways behind me.

'Hi, Donald.' The room responded, in chorus, before Donald continued.

'I am a vampire as you can see…'

'Pardon?' I mutter, under my breath.

'…and I also happen to be an alcoholic.'

'Alcoholics anonymous? I have two hours of sleep left and I was spending it in therapy?' I thought to myself…right before I made my way to the podium.

MOON

05:20

She would have started earlier but her mischievous laptop was in dire need of a reboot, according to HP maintenance support, and connectivity is priority over mental health. Plus, her idea of therapy was to pour words on a virtual imposter of the A4 paper. This way, her feelings live forever. Happiness, sorrow, comfort; all of them get to maintain their embers until the next time the universe decides to displace my apathy.

She sits up off the single bed that she hasn't had to share for a while, and as she leans against the wall behind her she slowly tucks her fingers behind the curtains of the window adjacent to her bed. Alora, sweeps them away in such a paced and elegant manner that the dust particles, illuminated in the candle light, appeared more animated than her.
Impatient with her own slowness, Alora tilts her head towards the right so she could see around the fabric and out of the misty window.

There he is. Alora smiles as if she had had doubts that he'd be there. She definitely didn't believe her eyes and the beauty they were beholding. She stared at the uneven cluster of silver in the sky; admiring the craters in his skin and wondering if this what her brain will look like, once the tumours are out.

Tonight, he is more luminescent than she can ever remember seeing him, but it may just be the sativa influencing her. Anxiously, she pulls the curtains close again; only a little to hide herself. Just enough to hide herself but he still shone through.

She smiles at herself and looks around sheepishly. No one else exists in her world – except for the him and her. Not even the stars came out to disturb their little love affair.

Exhausted from the flutters in her heart. She slides back under her quilt, and all of a suddenly she didn't need to write. Alora feels completely satisfied by her date with the moon. A strange rush flows to her head, urging her to tear down her curtains and just make him stay forever. She wanted him to fill him up with his light until she combusted. That way she wouldn't have to deal with the morning that is quickly approaching. Unfortunately, she is just as disillusioned about dying as she is about living a fulfilled life.

As a matter of fact, she began to feel bad about resolving to die – either from the surgeries or the chemo therapy.

'How lonely he will feel without me watching him'.

06:00

Alora watches God drag his paint brush across the sky. The pinks and oranges and reds are mesmerising.

He is still there, but not for long. His faint outline disappears behind a cloud. Alora knows he's still there but decide to shut her eyes before he completely disappears. She doesn't like goodbyes, so she leaves when he's not looking.

PASSION

I open my eyes, and in my mind, I turn around to enter into his warm aura

He's asleep but even in his unconscious, his heart beat directs mine

In one swift movement, I haul my heavy heart onto his and they join

A baseline incomparable

Perfect percussion

My mind is never as peaceful as when we make music with our bodies

Like last night when our moans harmonised

My heart skips a beat at the flashback, and he wakes up

He gasps and inhales my heavy presence, then sweeps my hair away from my neck

He buries his face in the fruity blast of smell that exudes from my skin

As he exhales and runs his fingers down my inversely arched spine I forget we're human

I float on the thrill, the moon tickles senses
It wont be up much longer

As a matter of fact as his eyes captivate me, he smiles
and I can feel the sun rising

I sit up gliding off his chest though I'm trying to savor
as much of his skin as possible

We're both upright and he stares at my body like
time's stood still

The sun's still rising but my shadow doesn't move
As I entwine my fingers in his my rhythm helps me
keep time

Seconds fly by but I'm static

Fireworks in my head, the sensation is only
quenched by a greater one as he grabs my thighs and
swings me

Like a precisely rehearsed routine he knows exactly
how to decrease the impact of my back hitting our
silk sheets

Prostrate he slides a limb under my back whilst two
of mine cross over behind his'

We skipped foreplay but the theatrics are in full
motion

We're rocking and rolling

On the waves of the ocean that is our bed

This man originates from its depths

He was built for passions I was built to receive

He grabs my hair and let's it veil his sleeve

As he heaves ho

To fro

Out of of control

And I...

Quiver

Shake uncontrollably

Make faces that embarrass me

But the best part will always be

Giggling furiously

And lying in each other's arms till we fall asleep

LOSS

Melanie was an anxious child. Too often, her siblings would hide one of the toys she had so perfectly arranged on her shelf. Toys that were never played with for fear that she'd dirty them. The only time her teddy bears were touched was when she needed to brush them. Her tea set was polished regularly. For her eleventh birthday, Melanie asked for wood polish for her doll house. She smiled regretfully at the new pink bicycle she was given instead, then bought it herself with two weeks' worth of her allowance. So when something was out of place, it was particularly distressing for Melanie. Growing up, she resented her family for trivialising her obsession and spent most of her time by herself until she became close to them again when she developed a fear of losing things.

On the few occasions that she went to social events, Melanie would often be found touching her earlobes every couple of minutes – checking that the earrings her mother gave her while on her death bed – the only earrings she ever wore – are still there. Since the day she broke down in front of her door because she couldn't find her keys in the chaos within her tote bag, Melanie only carries bags with enough pouches to accommodate everything individually.

Fortunately, Melanie's fear of loss didn't last very long. She hasn't been scared of losing things since she lost her mind.

One day, Melanie was tired. Her whole life her mind had been in overdrive. Every passing moment was riddled with worries she couldn't control. In the morning she worried about being late for work, at work she worried about deadlines. Her conversations with colleagues were careful and calculated, even when she had objections against the piles of paperwork that would be dumped on her, she bottled her anger out of fear of being laid off. She had children that didn't need her anymore, that she scrambled after like an ant on a sugar high. At night, she stayed up till the wee hours, thinking of why her husband was found, shot dead, in another woman's house. She was tired of not being able to control her thoughts so one Friday evening, when the kids were staying over at her sister's house, she called them to make sure they were ok. Melanie asked them what they ate and if they remembered to take any homework, that was due on Monday, with them.

Melanie took a long bath, something she hadn't done in years, put on the silk nightdress she wore on her wedding night and listened to Osibisa's *Welcome Home* as she moisturized her skin.

As she slipped into bed, with her favourite book in her hand, she scribbled 'I love you' at the bottom of the title page and slipped it in the drawer of her bedside table. On top of the table was the tramadol she faked months of excruciating period pain for.

She had long learnt to soldier through her endometriosis, but she knew her doctor was trigger happy with the opioid prescriptions. Because Melanie could never swallow pills, she had to spend some time opening the capsules and emptying the content into a wine glass. It was the last glass; the bottle was already empty.

When she was done, Melanie emptied a blister of six sleeping pills into her hand; appreciative of the fact that they were tiny. She swallowed them with a sip, smiled and then gulped down the rest of the wine, before tucking herself into her duvet. She was barely a few minutes into planning her own funeral when she slipped out of consciousness. Unfortunately, she woke up.

There is nothing more painful than when someone tells you they love you, but your brain doesn't have the information needed to recognize whether they are your brother or your husband. Some will introduce themselves but others suffer in silence. They will shoot at you, an unconvincing smile that masks the hurt they feel underneath at your bewilderment. As if, by denying them the recognition as your kin, you have betrayed some ancient code on which the universe depends. Melanie wished she recognized the names on her visitor's list when her nurse told them to her every morning.

Eventually, Melanie gave up. She was stuck between grateful that she survived a suicide attack and not remembering why she wanted to die in the first place. She would have memories of her childhood, but none of the people that claimed to be her family was in them. All she could ever remember was her young self and she didn't mind, after a while. Every day, she would wake up and think of those toys she took care of and it made her proud, how good she was at it. Her family got used to the fact that her brain periodically lost all her short-term memories and Melanie couldn't fret over losing things she didn't know she had.

Connect with the author online

Twitter: @okornore
Instagram: @okornore
Email: adjoamanu1@gmail.com

www.ingramcontent.com/pod-product-compliance
Lightning Source LLC
Chambersburg PA
CBHW020600160726
47991CB00002B/810